MW00882128

# 101 Coolest Things to Do in Lisbon

# Introduction

So you're going to Lisbon, huh? You lucky lucky thing! You are sure in for a treat because Lisbon is truly one of the most magical cities on this planet.

Around the city, you can find some of the most incredible galleries and museums in Europe, there is an abundance of food that will satisfy even the pickiest of palettes, there are green spaces and beaches just a stone's throw away, and shopping that is second to none.

In this guide, we'll be giving you the low down on:
- the very best things to shove in your pie hole, from typical Portuguese tarts and the best places to find them, all the way through to Michelin star restaurants
- the best shopping so that you can take a little piece of Portugal back home with you, whether that's in the form of some vintage clothes or a bottle of delicious port.
- incredible festivals, whether you want to rock out to incredible bands, or you fancy discovering independent Portuguese cinema
- the coolest historical and cultural sights that you simply cannot afford to miss from medieval castles through to museums dedicated to local history

- the best places to have a few glasses of port and party like a local

- and tonnes more coolness besides!

Let's not waste any more time – here are the 101 coolest things not to miss in Lisbon!

## 1. Get Acquainted With Fado Music at Clube de Fado

There is one type of music that is more popular than any other in Portugal, and that's Fado. The genre of music is normally mournful in tone, and has been traced back to the 1820s, but probably extends much further back in the country's history. If you would like to get better acquainted with fado music, there are countless places in Lisbon where you can enjoy a fado performance, but Clube de Fado might just be the best of them all. The club attracts some really big name fadistas, such as Cuca Rosetta and Mario Pacheco.

## 2. View the City from Lisbon's Majestic Aqueduct

Lisbon is a truly stunning city, and because the city can be quite hilly, there are many places and lookout points where you can take in a beautiful vista, but for us, there is one lookout point that offers a better view than all the others put together. The city has an incredible aqueduct called Aguas Livres. In certain parts of the city, its 119 arches dominate the skyline. The tallest arch has a height of around 65 metres, and walking along the arches offers an unparalleled view of both sides of the city.

### 3. Have an Artsy Day at the Centro de Arte Moderna

Arts lovers visiting Lisbon are in for a treat. While certain European cities such as Paris and Florence might be better known for their arts cultures, there is no shortage of museums and galleries to keep art lovers happy in the Portuguese capital. A visit to the Centro de Arte Moderna will give you a great opportunity to get to grips with $20^{th}$ century Portuguese artists, as well as international works from the likes of David Hockney and Anthony Gormley.

### 4. Sample the Famous Portuguese Custard Tarts

If there is one food that is most associated with Lisbon it has to be the custard tart. The custard is baked within flaky pastry, and the result is something simple but incredibly delish. While these custard tarts can be found all over the city, Pasteis de Belem is the bakery that is most famous for these sweet treats. You might have to wait a little while for a seat in this extremely popular café, but it will be well worth it. The bakery has been running for more than 150 years so they really know how to make a custard tart.

### 5. Visit a Stunning Gothic Tower, Torre de Belem

If there is one historic attraction that Lisbon is best known for, it is the Torre de Belem. Listed as a site of Unesco heritage, the fortress was built in 1515 as a way to guard the entrance to Lisbon's harbour. The fortress is symbolic of the country's age of discovery because it was the point of departure for global expeditions, and the first thing locals would see on their return. The stonework incorporates many motifs of discoveries, including a carved rhinoceros and historical beasts.

## 6. Take a Tour of the Picturesque Streets via Tram #28

As you wander around Lisbon, you are sure to notice that the tram is a very popular choice of public transport in the city. And, indeed, a tram ride is also something that every tourist should experience. The #28 tram line is particularly well known for passing through the most beautiful neighbourhoods, such as Baixa, Alfama, and Graca. It's also the best way of making it to the very picturesque but equally steep Alfama neighbourhood and to check out the view points without needing to make the steep climb yourself.

## 7. Feel Lisbon's Creativity at LX Factory

Lisbon has a wonderfully creative energy, and nowhere can you experience this with greater force than on a trip to LX Factory, a place where fashion, design, music, fine art, architecture, and communication converge. The LX Factory is a fun place to wander around on any day of the week, but it's every Sunday that the place really comes to life, because this is when its weekly market is held. If you want to find something extra special to take home with you, this is the place to find it.

## 8. Be Wowed by One of the World's Greatest Aquariums

When you think of Lisbon , you might not immediately think of nature and wildlife, but there is a heal of a lot of sea life surrounding the city on the coast, and a great deal of this is displayed in Lisbon's own aquarium, called the Lisbon Oceanarium. It is actually the largest indoor aquarium in all of Europe, and you could easily spend a whole day there. Some of the highlights include penguins, octopi, cuttlefish, seahorses, sharks, barracudas, and many other types of sea life besides.

## 9. Shop for Edible Souvenirs at Conserveira de Lisboa

A definite highlight of any trip to Lisbon is the incredible food. But if you don't want your culinary adventure to end, fear not because you can take plenty of delectable goodies home with you if you simply stop by the Conserveira de Lisboa. Located slap bang within the heart of Lisbon's downtown, you can find all manner of produce here. This place only sells canned fish, but trust us when we say that it does one thing very well indeed.

## 10. Drink Wild Cherry Liqueur at Casa de Ginja

If you like to have a wee tipple of an evening time, we have a feeling that you'll feel right at home in Lisbon where there are plenty of local drinks to wet your whistle. Of course, port is a great choice, but if you want to try something new and different, we can wholeheartedly recommend a glass of ginjinha, a local sour cherry liqueur. You'll find this around the capital city, but Casa de Ginja is particularly famous for this strong yet fruity drink.

## 11. Take a Day Trip to Magical Sintra

Okay, so Sintra actually lies a little outside of Lisbon, but this magical town is under an hour away by train and makes for the perfect day trip when you feel the need to get out of the city. It is often said that Sintra looks as though it is ripped from the pages of a fairytale, and that description couldn't be any more accurate. The highlight of the town is Pena Palace, a Romanticist castle that looks like something from a Disney movie.

## 12. Learn About Public Transportation in Lisbon

One of the reasons why Lisbon was able to experience such incredible growth as a European city was because of its very efficient public transportation system, which is in no small part because of the Carris company, which has its own museum in Lisbon. Inside this museum, you can trace the history of the company right back to its origins, and learn how public transportation in Lisbon has shaped the development of the city as a whole.

## 13. Purchase Trendy Cork Items From Pelcor

Okay, we know that you probably aren't visiting Lisbon to fill your suitcase up with cork related items. But if you do have a spare hour or two and you want to check out Lisbon's shopping scene, the Pelcor store, which specialises in cork items, is well worth a visit. If you have environmental concerns, you may be interested to know that cork is a very sustainable material, and a huge number of products can be made from the material. Inside the store, you'll find cork handbags, cork hats, and event cork umbrellas.

## 14. Wave a Rainbow Flag at Lisbon pride

Every June, the streets of Lisbon are completely taken over by a very special celebration: Arrial Lisbon Pride. Portugal is a country that has always been very progressive when it comes to LGBT rights, allowing both same sex marriage and same sex adoption. The annual Pride event is a celebration of these progressive rights and how much the LGBT community has achieved. There are tonnes of parties throughout the week, and the highlight is always the Saturday street parade, with tonne of colour, music, dancing, and glitter.

## 15. Watch a Film at the Indie Lisboa International Independent Film Festival

If you would like to discover the more underground side of Lisbon, take a break from the huge museums and galleries, and catch a movie at the annual Lisboa International Independent Film Festival instead. The main aim of the festival is to showcase exciting new films and directors that otherwise wouldn't have a platform in Portugal. As well as being able to watch some incredible films, there will be a selection of panel events, discussions, Q&As, and talks that you can purchase tickets for.

## 16. Visit one of Europe's Oldest Jazz Bars

If you have listened to just about as much fado as you can handle, and you'd like to spend an evening taking in some smooth jazz sounds, you are in luck because Lisbon is home to one of the oldest jazz bars in Europe: Hot Club. The bar has been entertaining locals and tourists since the 1950s. A recent addition to the space is a beautiful garden, and you can occasionally enjoy jazz concerts in the outdoors too.

## 17. Chow Down on Fish Stew at O Arrastao

While you are in Lisbon, you will want to eat as much seafood as you possibly can, and it doesn't get more local than a hearty fish stew. There are tonnes of places where you can eat very flavourful fish stew around the city, but we think that your Euros are best spent at a restaurant called O

Arrastao. The fish stew in this restaurant has even won local awards, to it's a great place to kick off a culinary adventure with an authentic taste of Lisbon.

## 18. Drink in a Traditional Portuguese Taberna

If you want to avoid the tourist traps and drink as a local person would on your trip to Lisbon, you need to head into the doors of the local tabernas. Our favourite of them all is called Taberna Portuguesa, and is located in the happening Bairro Alto neighbourhood. As the name would suggest, everything about this taberna is 100& Portuguese, from the interior décor to the plates of pica-pau, which are strips of delectable fried beef.

## 19. Sample Delicious Bites at Mercado de Ribeira

If you can't get enough market culture, Lisbon is a city that is sure to satisfy you, and the most impressive of all the markets is the Mercado de Ribeira. This market has its origins way back in the 13<sup>th</sup> century, and it was once one of the largest fish markets in all of Europe. Nowadays, the scale of the place is no less impressive, and inside you can find restaurants, stalls, and shops. Inside, Café de Sao Bento is the best place for a steak, and Garrafeira Nacional is an awesome place to stock up on Portuguese wine.

## 20. Buy Beautiful Candles at Loreto Candle House

Look, we know that you haven't trekked all the way to Lisbon to stock up on candles, but while you are in the city, we do honestly recommend a trip to Loreto Candle House, which is the premiere shopping destination for candles in the city. When you consider that this shop has been making and selling candles since 1789 and it's still going strong, you know that you are in the presence of candle greatness. As soon as you enter the store, you'll be hit by the aromas of citrus, roses, pomegranate, and many other gorgeous scents.

## 21. Enjoy a Mojito With a View at Sky Bar

In our opinion, Lisbon might just be the most picturesque capital city in all of Europe. With that said, the city is also very hilly, and it can be quite the workout to traverse some of the streets just to get a beautiful view. If you want to have a view without the hike, you need to know about Sky Bar. Set on the ninth floor rooftop of a five star hotel, this is the best place for a stunning view of the city while you have a mojito in your hand.

## 22. Try the Yummy Codfish Fritters at Taberna Tosca

While you're in Lisbon, it's imperative that you shove as much local food into your mouth as you possibly can, and a specialty that you really won't want to miss is the patanisca, which is essentially a salted codfish fritter. For our money, the best codfish fritters in the city can be found at Taberna Tosca, a tapas joint set within a beautiful historical building. If the weather is pleasant, be sure to snatch a table in front of the building in the open air.

## 23. Brush Up Your Portuguese Language Skills

Visiting Lisbon as an English speaker is really not too much of a problem. Most people have at least an intermediate level of English, and the people are friendly and helpful to boot. But it's always better if you can say some things in the local language, even if it's only the basics. That's why, if you're sticking around in Lisbon for longer than a couple of weeks, you should think very seriously about having some Portuguese lessons. The CIAL Centra de Linguas is our favourite classroom in the city.

## 24. Sample Food from Mozambique at Ibo

There is no shortage of wonderful and memorable restaurants around Lisbon, but one of the most special of them all has to be Ibo. This restaurant is set on the River Tagus, and you can experience a stunning view. Not just that, the food is incredible, and influenced by flavours from Mozambique combined with local flair. If you aren't sure what to order, we can wholeheartedly recommend the shrimp curry.

## 25. Be Wowed by the 16th Century Jeronimos Monastery

Dating back to the 15th century, the Jeronimos Monastery is one of the most stunning historical sights in all of Portugal. The monastery is so elaborate and ornate that this incredible building actually took over a century to build. The monastery is also very closely associated with sailors and explorers from Portugal, and, in fact, it was here that Vasco de Gama spent his last night before voyaging to the Far East. You can get there via public transport on the #15 tram.

## 26. Eat the Best Seafood of Your Life at Cervejaria Ramiro

There is tonnes of delicious food in Lisbon, but it's seafood that almost always steals the show. While there are plenty of places to eat yummy seafood in the city, we have a soft spot for Cervejaria Ramiro. The restaurant lies north of the city, but it's well worth the trek, and even Anthony Bourdain has recommended the place so it has to be something special. There's clams, shrimp, lobsters, and loads more deliciousness, plus a casual and fun atmosphere where the beer flows.

## 27. Take a Ride on the Santa Justa Lift

Something that you'll notice as you start to walk around Lisbon is that the Portuguese capital is a very hilly city indeed. The geographic dynamics make the city a truly stunning place, but strolling around can really put pressure on your knees and legs. One way of getting to a great height without needing any leg power is by utilising the Santa Justa elevator. The outdoor lift will take you all the way up to Carmo Square where you'll have an epic view of the city.

## 28. Buy Cool Design Items at Jardim da Estrela

If you like to experience some greenery while you are ion holiday, there are plenty of beautiful parks in Lisbon. Jardim da Estrela is one of the most popular of them all, but the locals don't only come here to enjoy the grass, trees, and sunny weather. In the spring, summer, and autumn, the park hosts a crafts and design fair on the first weekend of each month. This is a place where you can really feel the creativity of the city, and perhaps take home something special with you.

## 29. Enjoy a Cheap Lunch With a View at the Nuns' Canteen

The Nuns' Canteen is one of the best kept secrets of Lisbon, and it's one of the best places in the city for a cheap lunch with an awesome. The Nuns' Canteen earned its name because it is run by a Catholic association, and for just 8 euros, you can grab yourself a main course, a dessert, and a drink. The really great thing about the Nuns' Canteen is the incredible view that is offered up with your food. You get to look out at the glistening water of the river and the undulating streets of the city.

## 30. Have a Couchsurfing Adventure

When you visit a city for the first time, it can be a great idea to veer away from the tourist trail at least a little and experience things like a local person would. But how can you do this? Couchsurfing is a fantastic solution. With couchsurfing.com, you can find local people in Lisbon (and everywhere else in the world!) who have a spare couch or a spare bed and are happy to host people at no cost. Yes, this can be a great money saver, but it's the cultural exchange that is priceless. You'll get to experience first-hand how local people in Lisbon really live.

## 31. Try a Traditional Portuguese Cake Made With Almonds

If you have something of a sweet tooth, of course you are going to indulge in the famous custard tarts that can be found in bakeries around the city, but there are other desserts in Lisbon too. If you'd prefer to go for a slice of cake with your cup of coffee, you are in luck because Toucino de Ceu is a locally made cake that is difficult to tire of. This is a cake made from almond flour, and against all the odds, pork lard. Don't let that put you off – it's yummy!

## 32. Learn How to Cook Like a Lisbon Local

The food in Lisbon is nothing short of incredible, but isn't it going to be sad when you leave Lisbon and you can't eat the delicious salt cod, seafood, and custard tarts anymore? Well there is a solution. In the capital city, there are plenty of cooking schools where you can learn how to cook many of the dishes. We are particularly fond of Cooking Lisbon because they integrate trips to the market with cooking lessons, so you can explore the city and cook some delicious food all in one experience.

## 33. Hit a Few Golf Balls

If your idea of a perfect vacation is finding the local golf course and hitting a few balls, you are in luck because there are some really wonderful golf courses in and around Lisbon. Possibly the most famous course in the region is the Penha Longa Golf Club – a very upmarket golf course that has some fancy hotels situated nearby. The club attracts an elite set of golfers, and considering that this course has hosted the Portuguese Open, it also has a very esteemed reputation.

## 34. Treat Yourself to Portuguese Beers at Dois Corvos

When you think of European cities that are great for drinking beer, Lisbon almost certainly would not be the first city that comes to mind. With that said, there is certainly a beer culture to be explored in Portugal, but you need to do a bit of searching to find it. Around the city, you will often be served up beer in bottles, but in this lovely microbrewery there are twelve different beers on tap, and many of them are from Portugal so you can try the local specialties.

## 35. Indulge in a Selection of Sweet Treats at Tartine

If you have a sweet tooth, Lisbon is a dream city. There are bakeries and cafes all around the city that serve up the most incredible pastries and desserts, and one of the best places to indulge a sweet tooth is at Tartine. They sell the most picturesque fruit tarts, filled up with blackberries and strawberries that almost look too pretty to eat. They have also recently expanded into serving brunch and light lunches so it's a wonderful place to take it easy for a couple of hours.

## 36. Listen to Classical Sounds at Music Days Belem

Lisbon is one of the cultural capitals of Europe, and if you are fanatical about classical music, the city will serve you will at the Music Days Belem Festival, which takes place every

April. Across just three days, you can expect more than seventy concerts from both local musicians and musicians from around Europe and the world. There are also special concerts and activities for children, so the kids won't need to feel left out.

## 37. Cool Down With a Gelato From Santini

The summer months in Lisbon can be exceedingly hot, and if you are there during the summer, you'll want to take every opportunity to find shade and cool down. But, of course, the most fun way of cooling down is by indulging with a creamy scoop of gelato. For our money, the best place for gelato in the city is at Santini. As well as serving up delicious ice cream, this place is also a part of Lisbon's history as it was opened by an Italian immigrant in the 1940s. We particularly enjoy the sweet egg with pine nuts flavour.

## 38. Take in the Baroque Beauty of the National Pantheon

If you are in the east part of Lisbon, look to the skyline and you will be able to see the beautiful white dome of the National Pantheon, located in the picturesque Alfama district of the city. This important church dates back to the 16<sup>th</sup> century, but quite unbelievably was only completed in 1966. It is a possible to climb a flight of stairs up six levels to reach the very top of the church, and from there you will have the most magnificent view of the city.

## 39. Sip on Port in the Cellar of Solar do Vinho do Porto

If there is one local drink that you have to try while in Portugal, it is, of course, port. Port is a fortified wine that is made exclusively in the northern regions of the country, and it is generally much sweeter than regular wine, although there are many different types. If you want to get acquainted with port, Solar Vinho do Porto, is the place to do just that. Head into their cellar, and you'll be guided through an unforgettable port tasting experience.

## 40. Feel a Connection to Nature at Sintra Cascais Natural Park

Although Lisbon is not a super busy or polluted city, there might be times when you don't even want to see a building and would prefer to completely immerse yourself in nature. If that sounds like you, the Sintra Cascais Natural Park, which is less than an hour outside of the Portuguese capital, is the place for you to take a load off. There are plenty of well-marked hikes and cycle routes, so you'll have no problem embracing your inner adventurer.

## 41. Try the Portuguese Version of Surf n Turf

It seems as though every country in the world has its own version of surf and turf, but there is none more original nor tastier than the Portuguese take on a classic, which is called Carne de Porco Alentejana locally. The basic idea is that pork tenderloins are cooked with clams. The two ingredients complement each other perfectly, and the result is something rustic and yet decadent at the same time. Be sure to look out for this dish on local menus.

## 42. Have an Artsy Day at the National Museum of Ancient Art

Arts lovers on a trip to Lisbon need to etch in some time to visit the very impressive National Museum of Ancient Art. The museum was established way back in the 1880s, and since then it has established itself as a hugely important part of the city's cultural scene. The collection that has been accumulated over the years is extremely diverse, with textiles, sculptures, paintings, metalwork, furniture, and decorative art.

## 43. Relax in an Art Nouveau Café

There is plenty to see and do in Lisbon, but there are times when you will just want to relax in a comfortable chair with a strong cup of coffee or a relaxing tea. When that moment arises, we advise you to head straight to Café A Brasileira. This is actually the most historic café in all of Lisbon. It opened in 1905, and it has totally retained its art deco style with plenty of mirrors and black and white. The coffee is also very good.

## 44. Discover a Stunning Collection of 17th-19th Century Coaches

It might be a little bit hard to believe, but the Coaches Museum in Lisbon is one of the most visited sights in the whole city. While coaches is certainly a niche subject, the collection of 17th, 18th, and 19th century coaches here is actually the largest and most expensive collection of its kind anywhere in the world. Highlights from the collection include a vehicle used by France's King Louis XIV that has cherubs with bat wings, and a 19<sup>th</sup> century coach used by the Queen of England.

## 45. Learn About Portugal's Ties With Asia

Portuguese locals are fiercely proud of their heritage as explorers. It was the Portuguese that first had ties with Macau, and they also established the spice trade with India in Kerala and Goa so that Europeans could start to enjoy exotic spices. The best place to learn more about this part of the country's history and how it has influenced the present is at the Museum of the Orient. The Chinese screens and Ming porcelain on display is particularly impressive.

## 46. Grab a Drink at the Eccentric Sol e Pesca

There are plenty of places, and very nice places, to grab a drink in the Portuguese capital, but we have particular fondness for Sol e Pesca because of its quirkiness. The site of the bar and restaurant is an old fishing shop, and it still retains the look and the feel of the place. The wine list is really exceptional with all Portuguese wines, and it's also a great place to chow down on some of the famed canned fish from the area. Their own recipe books also make great souvenirs to take home with you.

## 47. Take a Journey Through Local History at the Lisbon Story Centre

If you are the kind of person who gets easily bored when hopping from museum to museum, you might find the Lisbon Story Centre a more intriguing and exciting museum prospect. This museum tells the story of the city from way back in medieval times and right up to the present day. But it does so in a highly interactive way, with an audio guide throughout that brings history to life. You can even experience the shaking of an earthquake that once brought the city to its knees.

## 48. Sample the Chocolate Cake at Landeau

Chocolate cake is one of those enduring foods that everybody in the world loves. If you want to find the very best chocolate cake in Lisbon, head straight to Landeau Chocolate. As the name of the café would suggest, the owners of the café are completely chocolate obsessed and know more than a thing or two about creating chocolatey goodness. The cake is thick and dense, so you only a need a small slice to satisfy a chocolate craving.

## 49. Get Back to Nature in Lisbon's Tropical Botanical Gardens

Although Lisbon can be pretty darn hot in the summertime, it's still not the tropics, but if you fancy pretending that you are somewhere tropical for an hour or two, you can't do much better than taking a stroll around the city's Tropical Botanical Gardens. Inside, you can even find some rare and endangered tropical plants and trees such as the monkey puzzle tree from South America and the dragon tree from the Canary Islands.

## 50. Sample Over 250 Portuguese Wines at Chafariz Do Vinho

While Portugal is better known for its port wine than its regular wine, there is still a huge amount of regular wine produced in the country every year, and wine lovers are sure to have a whale of a time in the Portuguese capital. One of the best places to sample a range of Portuguese wines is at Chafariz Do Vinho. In fact, at this bar hidden in the city's aqueduct, you can sample over 250 local wines, all accompanied by Portuguese tapas, so you will be spoiled for choice.

## 51. Immerse Yourself in Fado at Museu do Fado

If you have visited any bars at all during your time in Lisbon, you have no doubt already heard the legendary fado music, which the local people are so fiercely proud of. This experience is a great way of taking in fado, but if you want to learn more about this genre of music's origins, history and significance in the country, a trip to the Museum of Fado is well worth it. There is also an on-site record shop where you can purchase some fado of your very own.

## 52. Enjoy a Decadent Cocktail Night at CINCO Lounge

After a long day of sightseeing and walking from museum to museum, what you need is a strong cocktail. For our money, the best place to enjoy a couple of cocktails in a beautiful atmosphere is at the CINCO Lounge. The folks at CINCO are totally committed to using fresh ingredients, and believe us when we say that they are not scared of being generous with the alcohol. The port cocktails are a nice local touch.

## 53. Have Fun at the Interactive Knowledge Pavilion

If you are travelling with kids, it can be hard to know which attractions to take them to so they are kept engaged and are making happy memories throughout the whole trip. The Interactive Knowledge Pavilion is an interactive science museum that will capture the imaginations of your kids while giving them a learning experience at the same time. There is a particular focus on the way that technology is advancing and impacting on our everyday lives – something very pertinent to the young tech obsessed generation.

## 54. Take a Trip to the Beach of Cascais

Lisbon is a city that has beautiful weather year round, and fortunately, there is a beach close by so you can enjoy some of this weather while tanning on the beach. Via a direct train, Cascais is less than an hour away from the city centre, so it's perfectly feasible to pack a beach bag and enjoy a sunny beach day with your loved ones. Cascais is also a relatively upmarket area, so it's a fantastic place for discovering some great restaurants and boutique shops.

## 55. Enjoy Global Dishes at Mercado Fusao

While there is no doubt that the local Portuguese food served up in Lisbon is delicious, if you are staying in Lisbon for a longer period of time, you might want to expand your taste buds a little and try the global dishes that are served up at Mercado Fusao. The market is set outdoors, and there are food stands that represent cuisines from all over the world. Whether you like to chow down on Mexican tacos, soupy noodles from Thailand, or fiery curries from India, there will be something to suit your palette.

## 56. Indulge in Coscoroes at Christmas Time

The month of December is a particularly delightful time to be in Lisbon. The whole city is taken over by festive cheer, and there are also many culinary delicacies that only tend to rear their head at Christmas time. Something that we love to indulge with is coscoroes. This dessert snack that can be found in all the Christmas markets is really simple but really tasty. It's essentially fried pieces of dough that are given a fresh orange flavour.

## 57. Party Hard at NOS Alive

If you are interested in discovering Europe's summer festival scene, you might not have heard of any festivals in Portugal, but even if you haven't heard of NOS Alive, trust us when we say that it's a must experience for die-hard festival lovers. This music and arts festival has only been running since 2007, but since then it has gained a legion of fans who return every single year. Headliners in previous years have included Pearl Jam, The Beastie Boys, Bob Dylan, and Radiohead, so this is the festival for serious music fans.

## 58. Eat Seafood at Lisbon Fish & Flavours Festival

Lisbon is famous for its seafood, and while it's a very good idea to try the different dishes in various restaurants around the city, you can really elevate your seafood eating experience in Lisbon by experiencing the Fish & Flavours Festival, which is hosted in the city every April. The festival brings together some of the most celebrated chefs from the city as they showcase their most innovative and delicious seafood dishes to an audience of appreciative fish and seafood lovers.

## 59. Visit the World's Most Cutting Edge Book Shop

Ler Devagar, set within the funky space of the LX Factory, is more than just an ordinary bookstore. As soon as you walk through the doors, it's clear that the owners truly love everything about books, but it's also a place where you can catch a poetry reading, attend a concert, get a book signed by your favourite author, and even have a beer while you are leafing through a book's pages. The New York Times has even named it as one of the ten most beautiful book shops in the world.

## 60. Send Yourself to Pastry Heaven With God's Bread

Lisbon is one of the very best cities in the world for pastries, and if you fancy trying something new that's not just your standard croissant, we can heartily recommend trying Pao de Deus, which translates as God's Bread. The basic idea is that this is a brioche roll that is coated with a crunchy milk and coconut topping. It's great to eat just as it is, but many people fill it with ham and cheese to make a sandwich. That combined with coconut might sound strange, but it's honestly super delicious.

## 61. Enjoy the Shows at Festival de Sintra

While Sintra isn't a part of Lisbon proper, it is only an hour outside of the city by train, and it's a regular day trip for both locals and tourists. It's a fantastic town to visit at any time of the year, but it's particularly exciting to visit in May when the Sintra Festival takes place each year. This is a classical music festival, and the sublime architecture combined with soaring sounds of the orchestras is sure to transport you to another world.

## 62. Feel Festive at the Feast of St Anthony

The patron Saint of Lisbon is St Anthony, and that means the Day of St Anthony, which occurs between 12-14 June every year is a time of massive celebration in the Portuguese capital. And, of course, the main way that the locals like to celebrate is with an epic feast. There are many culinary treats to be had, but it's always the sardines that steal the show. In fact, the celebration is otherwise known as the Sardine Festival, and if you are in Lisbon at this time, you'll experience a 3 day frenzy of salting, grilling, and devouring delicious fresh sardines.

## 63. Party Til the Early Hours at Kremlin

Lisbon might be a cultural city, but that doesn't mean your trip has to be limited to museums and galleries. In fact, the

Portuguese capital also has a very well established party scene, and if you want to dance, dance, dance until the early hours of the morning, there are plenty of places where you can do exactly like that. We are particularly fond of a club called Kremlin because it's an "anything goes" type of place. Expect drag queens, freaks, and geeks, and everything in between.

## 64. Find Vintage Items at A Vida Portuguesa

Before you leave Lisbon, you will no doubt want to stock up on some beautiful items both for yourself and for family and friends. In our opinion, there is no better place than an old market called A Vida Portuguesa, a market where you can find carefully selected items that are truly a cut above the rest. Of course, you can find things like the typical canned fish of the region, but if you feel like spending more, you can also find handcrafted tableware, textiles, and other high end items.

## 65. Be Charmed by Marionette Puppets

Learning about Marionette puppets probably isn't going to be your priority on a trip to Lisbon, but if you find yourself in Lisbon on a rainy afternoon and you are struggling to find an indoor activity, the Marionette Museum is a wonderful place to pass a relaxed hour or two. The museum was created in

1987, and it is dedicated to showcasing the art of puppetry from all over the world. You'll be able to see puppets from centuries ago, and there is a particular emphasis on puppets from Portugal.

## 66. Have Bespoke Gloves Made at Luvaria Ulisses

As you walk around the city, you might notice that the people of Lisbon look effortlessly chic at all times. With boutique stores like Luvaria Ulisses, there is little wonder why this is the case. This is a shop that makes gloves, and sells gloves – nothing more than that. You can find gloves in a variety of colours and in seven different sizes and if you don't find something that immediately catches your eyes (unlikely story), you can have a pair made especially for you. The shop offers lifetime free repairs, which is a wonderful excuse to make a return trip to the city!

## 67. Try More Than 70 Gins at Lisbonita

When you think of gin, the first city that comes to mind is not going to be Lisbon. But if you are partial to a gin and tonic (and they do happen to go down very well in the Portuguese sunshine), the place to go is Lisbonita, a bar that specialises in gin. There are actually more than 70 gins behind the bar, and the staff really know their stuff, so don't be scared to ask them for recommendations. There's also Portuguese tapas on offer at the bar.

## 68. Buy Fado Records at Discoteca Amalia

Something totally unavoidable on a trip to Lisbon is the deep popularity of traditional fado music. Of course, watching fado shows in the local bars is a fantastic idea, but if you want to take a little bit of fado home with you, the place for this is Discoteca Amalia. This record shop is completely dedicated to fado music, and as soon as you enter Golden Street, where the store is located, you will hear the fado music blasting from the loudspeakers.

## 69. Sample Typical Portuguese Cheese From Manteigaria Silva

Foodies travelling to Lisbon will be in heaven in this European capital city. One of the shops where you can sample many local treats is the iconic Manteigaria Silva. The bacalhau and salt cod is very good, but the thing we like most of all is the typical Portuguese cheese called Serra de Estrela. This cheese is made from a breed of mountain sheep native to Portugal, and the cheese if so soft that it is almost spreadable. Delicious!

## 70. Discover Exotic Foliage at Jardim Garcia de Orta

Although Lisbon is not the kind of capital city where you will experience overwhelming amounts of hustle and bustle, there still might be times when you don't want to see any cars, any buildings, and you simply want to get back to nature. One of the most magical places to do just that is the Jardim Garcia de Orta. The gardens are named after a 16th century Portuguese naturalist, and you can find all kinds of exotic treasures on the grounds, such as Tabasco pepper trees and silk cotton plants.

## 71. Tuck Into a Warming Bowl of Caldo Verde

Okay, so chilly days in Lisbon are few and far between, but if you do find yourself in the Portuguese capital on a cloudy day and you want to eat some typical local comfort food that will warm your bones, Caldo Verde is what you need to be ordering every single time. Like most delicious foods, Caldo Verde is actually really simple – a soup that just combines potato, onion, olive oil, kale, and chorizo. It's particularly popular in fado bars across the city.

## 72. Be Totally Stunned by Lisbon Cathedral

If you are fanatical about religious architecture, you are sure to love your trip to Lisbon, and the jewel of the crown there is definitely Lisbon Cathedral. This Roman Catholic Cathedral is the oldest church in the whole city, dating way back to the 12$^{th}$ century. The church has changed over the centuries, and you can witness many styles within the one church. The façade is 12$^{th}$ century Romanesque, you can find a 14$^{th}$ century Gothic chapel inside, and there is also a lot of religious art from the 15$^{th}$ and 16$^{th}$ centuries inside.

## 73. Shop Organic at The Biological Market

If you are very choosy about the food you put into your mouth and you prefer to eat organic, you need to know about the Biological Market in Principe Real. The market takes place every Saturday, and farmers and producers from all over Portugal come to the market to sell their wares, which can include fruits, veggies, cereals, soaps, and more besides. While there, it's also worth strolling around Principe Park, and taking a moment to relax in one of the park's open air cafes.

## 74. Visit the Majestic Sao Jorge Castle

Something that you are bound to notice on the skyline as you walk around this picturesque city is the Sao Jorge Castle. This is a Moorish castle and its origins date way back to the medieval period of Portugal. As you ascend to the northernmost part of the city to visit the castle, you can appreciate what a great lookout point it would have been centuries ago as a defence of the port city.

## 75. Cross the Ferry to Eat at Ponto Final

Lisbon is a city that is cut into by the Tagus River, and it can be a great idea to take the boat trip to the less touristic side of the river if only to eat at the incredible Ponto Final restaurant. From the restaurant, you will experience breath taking views of both the river and the old town on the other side. And the menu is also something really special to boot. The speciality of the house is monkfish with rice, and it's totally delicious.

## 76. Take in a Concert at MusicBox

If your idea of a great night out is taking to the streets and finding somewhere to catch some live music, you are bound to fall head over heels for the live music culture of Lisbon. But if fado music doesn't quite do it for you, and you'd prefer to listen to something a little more contemporary, MusicBox is the place you need to know about. The venue lies directly underneath a bridge, and with its exposed brick and arches, it has a real underground, rock and roll feel to it.

## 77. Take Back Some Coffee from A Carioca

If you are a coffee lover, you are extremely lucky to be visiting a country like Portugal where the quality of the coffee is renowned around the world, and the people love to sip on coffee day and night. Of course, there are numerous cafes where you can enjoy a strong cup of coffee, but if you want to take some of that caffeine fuelled deliciousness home with you, A Carioca is the place to make a purchase. This place has been the premiere destination for local coffee lovers since the 1930s, so you can be sure that you'll be purchasing high quality product.

## 78. Enjoy all the Beauty at the Museum of Decorative Arts

Portugal is a country that is full of beauty, and this is not least because of the strong culture of decorative arts in the country and its former colonies such as Macau. One of the best ways to experience all of this beauty in one place is by visiting the Museum of Decorative Arts. Inside, you will find more than 1300 items of display, which are hugely varied. You'll discover local tile work, Chinese porcelain, old books, silverware, and much more besides.

## 79. Attend an Experimental Jazz Festival

Everybody knows that fado is the music genre of choice in Lisbon, but if you prefer the smooth sounds of jazz, all is not lost. At least not if you time your trip to coincide with the Jazz Em Agosto festival in the month of August. This experimental jazz festival is one of the most acclaimed jazz festivals in all of Europe, and each year, jazz talent both local and from around the world is attracted to the Portuguese capital to perform.

## 80. Climb to the Top of Santa Marta Lighthouse

On a trip to Cascais, which lies just an hour outside of the Portuguese capital city, one of the highlights of any visit is a trip to the Santa Marta Lighthouse. Constructed in the 1860s, this 25 metres tall lighthouse still guards over the River Tagus today. If you climb to the top of the lighthouse, you'll experience a beautiful vista of the surrounding area, and if you have time, do check out the museum inside the lighthouse as well.

## 81. Eat Cheap Seafood at Sea Me Quiosque

Most people know that Lisbon is an awesome city for seafood lovers, but most tourists don't venture too far away from the tourist restaurants. These often serve up some nice dishes, but they won't give you the local experience, and they're not an option for budget travellers. For cheap, delicious seafood where you'll see a long line of locals, Sea Me Quiosque is the place to be. This very simple street vendor by the sea offers a yummy fish soup for less than 3 euros!

## 82. Check out Islamic Art at Museu Calouste Gulbenkian

If you are the kind of person who loves to hop from museum to museum on a trip abroad, Lisbon will be right up your street, and a museum that art lovers will fall head over heels from is the Museu Calouste Gulbenkian. There is a huge array of artwork in the museum. You can find art from the Greco-Roman period, Egyptian Art, and Armenian Art, but the highlight has to be the wonderful array of Islamic and Persian art on display.

## 83. Sample a Local Tipple – Vinho Verde

It is no secret that Lisbon is a city of wine lovers. You might be expecting to sip on port, a type of fortified wine, day of night, and while this is certainly an option, you should also take the time to sample the less talked about Portuguese wine, Vinho Verde, literally translated as green wine. These wines are younger than ordinary wines, which makes them lighter and sweeter, and perfect for a summer picnic in the city.

## 84. Take Surfing Lessons

When you visit a European capital city, you probably don't expect to be trying your hand at very many water sports. But actually, Lisbon is the perfect place if you want to combine culture with adventure. If you have never tried your hand at surfing in the open sea before, your trip to Lisbon could change all of that. Lisbon Surf House lies just 10km outside of the centre of the city, and it's a great place to stay if you want to meet other adventurers and hit those waves.

## 85. Eat at a Michelin Star Restaurant

Your vacation is the time to splurge, indulge, and enjoy yourself without a thought for the consequences, and that means sometimes you have to bite the bullet and book a table at a fancy restaurant. There are plenty of great restaurants all over Lisbon, but maybe Belcanto with its Michelin star is the most acclaimed of them all. The suckling pig with orange puree is a total revelation, but truthfully, you'd be hard pressed to find anything that disappoints on the menu.

## 86. Purchase the Fanciest Chocolate Bars in Portugal

The local population sure does love chocolate, and if you love everything chocolate related just as much, we can recommend a trip to Bettina & Nicol Carollo so that you can really indulge that sweet tooth of yours. This family run chocolatier creates thin artisanal chocolate bars with delicious flavours like sea salt, ginger, pepper, sesame, and orange. All of the cacao beans are roasted in house so you get a fresh and flavourful product every time.

## 87. Go Birdwatching at the Tagus Estuary

Although Lisbon is a very much a cultural city, if you are a nature lover, we don't think that you'll be disappointed by a trip to the Portuguese capital. The Tagus estuary offers the water, plant life, and climate that so many different species of birds love, and that makes it a wonderful spot for birdwatchers and nature lovers in general. In fact, you can find more than 250 species of birds, including flamingos and little bustards.

## 88. Pass a Couple of Hours at the National Azulejo Museum

As you stroll around the city, you are certain to notice all of the stunning tilework, which you can see on the inside and outside of many buildings. Portuguese tile has a specific style that is tin glazed, and the name of this is Azulejo. It's a pleasure to spot these tiles around the city, but if you really want to immerse yourself in it, a trip to the National Azulejo Museum is a great idea. The exhibitions are set out in chronological order, and you can find everything from the 15<sup>th</sup> century to the present day.

## 89. Get Back to Nature at Tapada Nacional de Mafra

If you feel like escaping the city for one day and to immerse yourself in nature, an incredible park called Tapada Nacional de Mafra lies just one hour outside of the city, and it's a place where you won't see any buildings or hear any cars, but be completely immersed in nature. There are a number of established paths through the park so you can enjoy hikes without fear of getting lost, and you can even enjoy horseback rides on the weekends.

## 90. Start Your Day With a Coffee From Pois Café

If you are the kind of person who can't think about starting their day without a caffeine hit, you will positively adore Pois Café, which is widely acknowledged by locals as having the best coffee in a coffee loving city. If you feel like taking a seat and sticking around for a while, you should know that they also serve up great breakfasts. And if you can manage caffeine in the evening, you might want to stop by later in the day when they often showcase live jazz performances.

## 91. Take in a Show at the National Theatre of Sao Carlos

There are tonnes of great museums and historical sights dotted around Lisbon, but what are the things you can do to keep you occupied in the evening time? If you love any excuse to get all dressed up, we'd totally recommend booking tickets for a show at the stunning National Theatre of Sao Carlos. This opera house dates way back to the 18th century, and the building is one of the most beautiful in the city. You can find incredible opera, ballet, and classical music performances, so be sure to keep your eyes peeled on their programme of events.

## 92. Indulge a Sweet Tooth With Bola de Berlim

There are few foods more comforting than a soft and squishy doughnut that is still warm from the deep fat fryer. Practically every country indulges in doughnuts of one variety or another, and the Portuguese doughnut is called Bola de Berlim. These pastries are normally larger than your typical doughnuts, which is no bad thing, and they are filled with a rich custard made with egg yolks.

## 93. Find Something Special at the Feira da Ladra Flea Market

If you are the kind of person who loves to rummage around for special items, you are sure to find something extra special at the Ladra Flea Market. This is actually the oldest market in all of the city, with origins that date back to the Middle Ages. This is a street market where anything and everything can be found at a stall, in a tent, or simply spread out on the pavement. You'll be able to find old cameras, prints and art work, design items, used furniture, antique jewellery, and much more besides.

## 94. Indulge Your Inner Fashionista at MUDE

Do you fancy yourself as something of a fashionista? If so, a trip to MUDE (its full name is Museu Do Design e Da Moda), needs to be right at the top of your Lisbon agenda. Set within a former bank, this is one of the world's leading museums for 20th century design. Inside, you can find more than 1000 design objects, and more than 1200 garments from the likes of high profile designers like Jean Paul Gaultier, Vivienne Westwood, and Yves Saint Laurent.

## 95. Eat the National Dish, Bacalhau

If you only try one local dish in Portugal, it simply has to be bacalhau. Bacalhau is very simply the word for cod in Portuguese, but in the context of visiting Lisbon, it will always mean dried and salted cod. There are actually 365 different ways of cooking bacalhau, one for every day of the year, so there is bound to be a type to suit your palette. The history of this dish dates back to the 14$^{th}$ century in Portugal, so tucking into this dish is also to taste an aspect of the country's history.

## 96. Learn About the Local Seafaring Heritage at Museu de Marinha

The local people in Lisbon are fiercely proud of their country's heritage as a seafaring nation that has made many important discoveries, and as a result, the Maritime Museum is one of the most important museums to be found in the city. There are a staggering 17,000 items on display within the museum, and some of the highlights include two 18$^{th}$ century ceremonial barges and a display of 15<sup>th</sup> century Japanese armour.

## 97. Rock Out at Super Bock Super Rock Festival

If you love nothing more than to have a serious rocking out session with awesome live guitar bands, you need to know all about the Super Bock Super Rock festival, which is one of the premier rock festivals in all of Europe, and is hosted in Lisbon every year in the middle of July. Some of the acts that have performed at the festival in previous years include Bloc Party, Iggy Pop, Massive Attack, and Kendrick Lamar.

## 98. Drink Caiparinhas on the Street in Bairro Alto

One of the truly awesome things about Lisbon is that it is totally legal to drink on the street, and the climate makes it appropriate to do exactly that during every single month of the year. Bairro Alto is a trendy little neighbourhood with lots of small bars that sell caiparinhas in plastic cups. The truth is that it really doesn't matter where you purchase your cocktail, because everybody invariably ends up drinking on the streets together. It's a fantastic way of making new local friends.

## 99. Delve Into the Past at the Nucleo Arqueologico Museum

This small archaeological museum is somewhat overlooked in the regular Lisbon guides, but we reckon that it's totally worth a visit, particularly if you want to explore local history. On the museum tour, you'll actually be guided downwards into an Iron Age archaeological site. Unbelievably, you will even be able to visit a Roman sardine factory that dates way back to the 1st century. You'll also see Lisbon's only Roman mosaic, which dates back to the 3rd century. History buffs will be bowled over.

## 100. Dance the Night Away, the Gay Way

Lisbon is a super gay friendly city, and even if you aren't gay yourself, you are more than welcome to party hard with the local LGBT community. Trumps is the main gay club in the city, and it's a place where you can let your hair down, and dance to cheesy pop music whoever you are. The club doesn't tend to fill up until at least 2am, so this isn't the place to be if you are looking for an early night!

## 101. Discover the Street Art of the City

Lisbon has a vibrant and dynamic arts culture, but you only get to see one side of the arts culture if you confine your arts experience to galleries. Lisbon also has a vibrant street art scene, and all you need to do to discover it is take a walk around the city! If you take the Graca Literary Walk, you can see many murals adorning the walls. Some of them are political, and some are simply beautiful.

# Before You Go...

Thanks for reading **101 Coolest Things to Do in Lisbon**. We hope that it makes your trip a memorable one!

Keep your eyes peeled on **www.101coolestthings.com**, and have a great trip!

**Team 101 Coolest Things**

Made in the USA
Middletown, DE
15 December 2016